STILLS

MARK PARSONS

STILLS

MARK PARSONS

SOUTHERNMOST BOOKS
Saint Augustine, FL 2023

For more information: SouthernmostJournal@gmail.com

Published by Southernmost Books
Saint Augustine, FL

First Edition
ISBN: 979-8-218-25653-1

Typeface: Avenir

Cover and interior design: Gavin Stephen Lambert III

Cover art: Gavin Stephen Lambert III

...Is A Tired Old Woman

I. Beading the Dome

II. In The Neck

III.   Coils

Worth: There is no conspiracy. Nobody is in charge.
It's a headless blunder operating under the illusion
of a master plan.

Cube (1997)
Dir. Vincenzo Natali

Fascination and Dread
An Introduction
Mark Parsons

Arthur Rimbaud wrote, "'I' is someone else." With regard to Henry, the protagonist of *The Dream Songs*, Berryman observed: the speaker bares a strong resemblance to the poet. The speaker of these poems is a cipher that exists to name and register the world, an extension of the poet's soul, the spiritual life of the poet projected outward, a visionary dream-world. Berryman used artifice to model the world, self-consciously imposing personae and inventing speakers, all of who were refracted aspects of Henry's mind. The speaker in these poems is irresistibly drawn to uncover what's beneath the dream, even as he's anxious and filled with dread and foreboding.

These poems are not confessional. All art, in fact all making, or *poiesis*, is a confession. Pound observed some poems assume form as water conforming to the shape of a container, and others do so as a tree has form. These poems assume form as a concentration, a reduction, a distillation of the artist to his essences. Doing so, the poems reveal the truth of the poet's soul back to him.

In his essay on Benjamin Franklin, D.H. Lawrence wrote "[the] soul is a vast [..] dark forest. The Hercynian Wood that scared the Romans so [...] Who knows what will come out of the soul of man? The soul of man is a dark vast forest, with wild life in it." In the sequel to *Ghost in the Shell*, the movie that inspired *The Matrix*, Mamoru Ishii has a character observe, "If the essence of life is information carried in DNA, then society and civilization are just colossal memory systems." Moving through the world of the poems like a ghost in a landscape, the speaker inhabits his memory with a mixture of fascination and dread.

I.   Beading the Dome

Your Face Burns My Hands

The woman on a bench across the street
fingers a lock of her red hair.
She straightens a forelock that hangs from her temple,
to examine the ends
like the dagger point of an artist's brush.
Rubbing her fingers together
she carefully
and self-consciously
lays an auburn tress on the bench.
The scissors make crisp and decisive shearing sounds.
Twirling each lock at the edge of her vision, she cuts flush to pale scalp.
Today isn't windy.
The pile of hair beside her drifts
between the wooden slats, catching hints of sunlight.
A man in a grey boilersuit
rounds the corner and passes the scaffold.
Stops at a tree
planted in the sidewalk.
He shakes a can and sprays black spots
on the trunk below the branches.
The leaves are green and thick, the only things
reflecting light
anywhere on the street.
The man replaces the white cap
and walks to the next tree, past the woman,
who continues to cut.

Reflected in a shop window
I see the doorway over my left shoulder, framed
with tiles of white and blue:
someone dressed in chinos starts down
the narrow stairs inside, and turns and goes back up.
I can't remember why I'm here, neither
the reason I came nor the reason I stay—I forgot,
or never knew.
A rind of white where the woman
has cut away around her ear, she gathers a long tress
off her collar. Her head at an angle,

the man in a jumpsuit
walks past,
shaking the can as he looks at the back of her
head in the shop window.
The next tree is the last one on the block.
The woman runs her hand
over the newly-shorn side of her head,
copper strands wound tight around her fingers.
Between the man and the woman,
the bus shelter.
Standing before the final tree,
the man
shielding his eyes
with his hand as he sprays.
And again,
several inches lower.
The hem
of her print skirt
flutters away from her knees,
which are pink.
Both of them.

Dismember, Or the Swimmer at Land

A terrestrial caliper made out of spits
banded orange, yellow, and wheat diffracts water
lapping at your bare feet,
breaking on the pointy algae-slick rocks.
Between the landmass barriers presenting layered sediment
a Bermuda-rigged sloop at full sail drifts.

The earthly armature, curving away from you
like vintage antique ice block tongs,
pinces blue that dissolves to a haze of vapor and light.

This cove is a category
the distance of what's not
let waves in to carve as outline
in softer rock.

Lichen-covered outcrop jutting overhead, the idea
of what is not
wheels around you like you are the fulcrum.

Here at the diffraction limit
of softer rock
that became what is not, an evergreen
sapling strains to grow out of a cleft splitting an outcrop.

From a cut on the bottom of your foot blood runs
and flows down over granite shapes
peaks of water in piston lockstep imitate,
issuing forth from where the sailboat drifted into strata.

You aren't far from where you're supposed to be.

Voix Acousmatique Overheard by a Pilgrim with Skin in the Game

A kindred soul you meet
half-way
to who knows where,
easy to recognize when it happens
because there's always two of you, a partner so
both of you can be at the mercy of the other's character defects:
you may not know
you're meeting the ghost of your destiny
on the last leg of his return.

Caravan

"One does not become enlightened by imagining figures of light […] but
by making the darkness conscious."
—Carl Gustav Jung

1. Supplicate

Don't believe in the myth of the wise old woman
confined to a wheelchair and taking the air at the end of a pier,
who will draw you up out of this silence
that's all you can hear,
to a surface above
you can only imagine like bait
deep in the water

and quilt you in the geometric pattern
spread out upon her lap.

Somewhere beyond this darkness you believe
is light, there is light, and you are here, at the predawn center,
waiting for day to ascend panoramic
urban skyline
circumscribed like the view
from the bottom of an abandoned well.

The space you're in
shudders,
and you see its surface
at last.

2. Travelers Dream about the Peasants

I wake up and see my wife
sanding her elbow
at the opposite end of our berth.

Dreamily
she announces to nobody
in particular,
"It's a callous," and sighs,
making a sound like the brakes that exhale on a semi.

Every day we wake up in a different carriage.
We're like a blossom on a branch.
No…
we're like an amber bar of soap.

She crumples the oval.
Before she scuffs away
I hear her say "jacquard."

A zebu mounted on a hill
in the distance, the electric shaver
buzzing like an angry insect.

Our compartment spins out,
but the train hasn't moved.

3. The Holding Tank

Sitting hunched in the kitchen chair,
thick, wet braid
of straw
yellow hair, woven
tighter than wick for a hurricane lamp,
tapered
to a dagger point
like an artist's brush, bristles
dipped in paint,
on the narrow 'v' of your collarbones,

don't ask me who you are.
If you want to know,
ask yourself
what you were doing there.

You forgot what to do,
when what
was the case was the case,
and unfit
to make contact
came to,
where we were certain to find you.
Not letting you dry off or even change your clothes,
that are wet,
I start with the questions.

This hall, the door,
the bed, and bed side table, chair and chest of drawers,
the physical dimensions of the room:
you can't help but know there's a reason why
you feel small.
That reason has been here. That reason is out there.

Blue Cannibals

Raincoat tied at the waist and buttoned,
the woman shifts as I sit down
directly across from her, folded in thirds
newspaper under my leg.
Take the cigarette.
Shaking the purple disposable lighter
next to her ear she listens.
The meshwork
that lines the chainlink distended.
"Hope you aren't late, but he's always a quarter of
Tuesdays."
Exhale. A line of ants
red on the concrete in sunlight
from under her bench
and "you make that?" as smoke
over black swells of mesh windscreen drifts,
sucked out bright empty blank
doorway. She steps
to the plexiglassed-in map.
A red mark of egg shape on pale calf.
A yellow plastic
cup skids along the gutter.
I mash the ember under my heel.
Tuck
what's left
behind my ear.

Still Life with Human Beings

The parquet missing a few teeth.
Our parrot gnaws the sinewy bars of its cage
with a blue beak. My wife
emerges from the closet stooped
like a migrant worker with a short-handled hoe.
I point to the radio burning on the porch.

"You field tool," she hisses
and my eyes begin to water.

Kneeling beside a cardboard box
scrawled with numbers
in red lipstick,
my wife
gathers up her apron and prairie skirt
and starts to push the box
through a doorway
suited only
to very small children,
crawling after
until she's swallowed up by nylon garment bags.

I remember the closet is deep:
the deepest closet in our house is here in the front hall.
Crouching at the entrance,
I hear the periodic scoot of cardboard on linoleum.
Then my wife's voice,
her Czech accent so thick, her speech
labored, self-conscious,
like every word is a toilsome, alien thing,
like she's regressed
to when she was seven, the age she first
spoke, her dentist drunkenly confided,
pulling me off to the side at our wedding reception.
And then a different voice,
a man's I recognize from dreams
says, "What a thief he was."

Poached

SEALs used to call Green Beret colonels "green wings."
Caravaggio sucked; I mean, he was
a terrible painter.
Groups in particular. X-rays
reveal in dramatic religious depictions
completely distinct paintings
under the usual ones art historians venerate.
One of these
"other" compositions
detected by the naked eye is called pentimento,
a persistent, ghost-like image.
The husband of the woman in the apartment below and one over,
a SEAL for forty months in Vietnam
and later, after they "shut the war down," an expat merc
and one of Uncle Sam's Bad Boys,
says the most authentic movie ever made about the war is *The Siege
        of Firebase Gloria.*
The man who plays the sergeant, Lee Ermey,
also had similar roles in *The Frighteners* and *Full Metal Jacket.*
Ermey was in real life
a Marine and non-commissioned staff officer.
At the first of two parties I've been to since I moved here
I met a woman and her name was Gloria.
She asked how I liked being here. I said I was homesick.
She said, "Oh
you were born in the desert?" and I said, "No,
I was born in Kentucky."
An army brat, she didn't understand about rednecks.
The first of a number of conflicting explanations with regard to the word
"redneck," is the necks of hippies
were white and tender due to their long hair and burned
after marching all day on parade grounds in the brutal and exhausting
lens-like combination of humidity and blazing sunlight
common to places like Parris Island
in South Carolina and Fort Benning in western Georgia.
Another explanation is in small, rural communities throughout the south
parents disciplined their children
with slaps on the backs of their necks, which turned

the necks a near permanent shade
of iridescent pink.
A third, more widely accepted account
Maintains the word refers to anyone who works outdoors,
laboring in farm fields, where exposure to direct sunlight, along with hats
          that shelter faces,
and clothing with loose and open collars
gives the person—after years of getting sun-burned—darkish, crusty red skin.
When Gloria visited my office later
to pick up some materials she wanted to use in her class
she asked if these readings were part of a canon.
I said, "I just read everything."
She said, "I thought you were a redneck."
I said, "I never fit in there."
Then she said, "Oh."

Arboreal Is as Close as I Can Get to Her

In her former life
a fly-fishing guide, smoked
filterless cigarettes.

A guy who used to live in Venice Beach
says, "She would have fit in," where he no longer is.
She wasn't always quite so glamorous.
We both look straight ahead, at the mirror behind the bar.

Metal flash of a barbell stud
in the damask rose of her mouth, she laughs,
and it makes me feel like I kissed a ten-year-old boy.

Perched on the lid of the cooler
that's kept stocked with bottles of anise and caraway
seed liquor,
turning her head to the side
so her face is in profile, she presses an ear
to the mirror and listens to
the warm glass,
the decrepit reflection it casts,
and she's able to hear the stampede of the narcissists
coming to mourn her.

Untitled

Reflected at one end,
where the sidewalk rises on an oak root,
that oak. Three kernels

drying where water was—a dark rind
of lung shape. A squirrel
leaps
from a milky bough.

The van with primer spots
u-turns.
Cruises back.

Behind him. She walks down
steps of wine-red tile, mortar white as bone.
Her hand
shuttles over black rail.
Drops of water drip beneath her fingers,
catching warp threads of sun between slender cast iron balusters.

The Story of the Matte Kind, or Road

Thicket and undergrowth backlit like crêpe paper
you could poke your finger through,
make a hole to the other side of what you can't be sure
licks green prehensile tongues that drift
up to leafy canopy.
This vaulted stained-glass blaze constricts the asphalt road,
interlocking angular
crushed stone
faces stuck of a piece with bitumen
winding tar
glazed over terrain
I can't see,
feel disconnected from
like I myself am rising up by licks
higher and higher until
finally
floating, ethereal,
undulant river of blacktop absorbing
all the available light, making me wonder about
what's underneath.

Tuning

He needs to be unconscious first,
before you start. For this
you can
use the lug wrench
you keep behind your seat.
Holding the L-shaped tool by its blade end,
your grip firm,
your wrist relaxed,
your arm
free-flowing,
strike his temple,
above the ear, and then wait
for the handle to quit
vibrating,
for the overtones
of a sudden act of violence
to die away
before you move—
Next empty your victim's pockets, putting
all that you find in your pockets
to ensure
little is lost as you strip him
naked, and put his clothes in your el Camino.
You're almost in the clear.
You've learned how to leave your best friend concussed,
naked and broke in a ditch by the interstate
in November. You will know to
travel accompanied only by strangers.

The Tang

Celery ribs and pimento-stuffed olives, all there is at my house to eat. So I drive to the mall, where an aerobics class giving a demonstration has attracted a crowd big enough to clot the corridor. Squeezed between the back row of spectators and grimy marble wall, I emerge but only to have a couple of guys I've never seen before pelt me with quarters from the entrance to one of the anchor stores. I want to tell them their days are numbered. However, by the time I reach the entrance they're gone. I'm browsing the sweatpants and thermal underwear when the same two guys jump me and start dragging me through the store. I'm struggling, I'm putting up a fight—I mean, why deny it? And we all end up on the floor. Curled up in a ball under these two strangers, I unsheathe my knife: it's a Bowie knife, enormous, gleaming. The handle warm in my hand, I lunge and stab and swing. I'm trying to hit anything I can sink the knife in up to the fist my hand makes around the handle. I hear a crack, splitting bone, and—the blade stuck— pull back hard. I'm really going at it: the silken action of my arm drawing back and releasing, over and over, seduces me. What if an errant swing of the fearsome blade finds me? I wonder. The point clinks against something like metal or stone, and florescent shards rain down in darkness. And so many bodies. It's no longer just us, this tangle of flesh. Fabric tearing, I pull the knife through whatever it's caught in: the serrated edge on the back of the blade doing the work for which it was forged.

II. In the Neck

Mary and Barb Get Divorced

The sooty water churns,
marbled with foam that reticulates lace.
We've been in the water
seven minutes;
something like silt or grounds
fastens collars around our necks of high, black rims.
An ashen swipe on Tyler's chin,
our faces streaked. The salesman squeezes in,
shoving me over a nozzle that gouges a watery jet in my flank.
Trying to make a little room
I look up at Tyler.
Mary says she doesn't want a drink without booze
till she's the hell out of French Lick—away
from the goddamn smell of sulfur!
I rest my head against bullnose cement,
and close my eyes:
the sound of the motor pours in my ears
like something wet, and breaks up like gravel in a tumble dryer.
A bead of moisture trickles down my face.
The salesman puts his hand
on my shoulder;
we've been in the bath long enough.
Standing under shower heads, their pale bodies stream grit.
Coming here this morning,
Mary gets lost in the national forest.
She is so upset
that we have to stop.
I drive to a diner for directions.
While I'm inside,
Mary puts the top down,
walks around to the driver's side
and gets in the car.
The charcoal leather exhales in sunlight.
The red paint—so red I feel weak.

Broadside

The polar bears captured as juveniles
during an episode of *Wild Cargo*
just after the first years of their young lives
when they were dependent on the mother for survival
along the northern coast of Greenland
yellow now, fully-grown,
taller than generals,
intent on red
puncture-proof rubber balls
smeared with peanut butter, skidding over simulated ice floes:
the bears' condition not that bad,
considering humans—maybe they were Puerto Ricans—
are harder to digest than fish,
even street urchins
skipping school, stripped to white cotton brief underwear
on a fledgling and untested macho dare
beside the tank.
Such is the problem with childcare in poor ethnic neighborhoods...

The director, producer and star of *Wild Cargo*,
told by a journalist
while being interviewed for *Playboy* magazine
he was rumored to be on the kill list of a third world dictator
who possessed
hundreds of hours of the filmed expeditions
as well as some natives
imprisoned for having been saved by this white man
for whom they'd been working as porters and guides—
he says there's no hereafter, what matters:
faster airplanes, bigger crocodiles, and younger women.
This doesn't mean
soaring rates for jet insurance
doesn't have some very far-reaching importance,
or anyone who says he's not afraid
looking out a cockpit to see an engine on fire
isn't a fool and liar—
but walking into a restaurant in Las Vegas
to the palpable electric

charge in the air
as a hundred men turn as one
and give a standing ovation to his much younger wife
makes it worthwhile.
After all,
to lead the orchestra
you must turn your back on the audience.

First Course in Etiquette

Our heads lolling about Marie and I come to
squinty-eyed and blinking.
We clack through the lobby and out the pneumatic,
hermetically sealing,
matched swinging doors.
Noonday sun
glares from cars
parked along the boulevard.
It's the first
time in our squalid disposable lives
that Marie and I
both use our best manners.
An offshore breeze
kicks up.
I lose my footing and stumble,
Marie's forest green skirt
lashes my face.
A paltry average, next to a giantess like Marie I'm very small,
and strangers stare at us from shady porticoes,
still and colorless as statues:
great lamps where birds have nested swaying high above.
Someone's child
loses its way in the hem of Marie's skirt
and I guide it out,
my hand on its soft head.

The Renowned Cinematographer Shows Off on His Honeymoon

The rusted sugar mill the road we're on winds past
          in lush vegetation
breathes out processed cane, distracting me from
          the woman sitting beside me, who's driving our rental over
patchwork asphalt our car tires lick
          like a pack of dogs, winded after a grueling run.

Magnum P.I. was produced
here on this island, the ludicrous image of giant Tom Selleck
peering over his Ferrari's tiny sloping windshield
gives way to thoughts of where this woman and I have been
together, and where we may yet go, each on our own.

I could swear off Fay Wray,
but that's not been the situation for so long…
anyway, such a flimsy vow
I'd just concede to a petulant child, should reference
Johannes Vorster, who had a penchant for the movies of John
          Ford, and thought
every movie house in Capetown showing Ford's flicks
seven nights a week the finest propaganda, kept the natives in line.

The sweet, iron-rich air
of the mill replaced:
motor oil
from a broken seal
drips to streak the valve cover,
burn under red hood.

Security

The closed-circuit TV
dome camera
from drop ceiling tile grid
watches the curious thing as it happens
below: women who work
the checkout lines,
gathered together in small groups,
pull from identical smocks in the company's colors
smartphones to log in and check
their preferred
social media websites for updates,

an unthinking gesture
        taken up
woman by woman and
        traded off,
checking what
        they last knew

        against what they know now:
staying abreast of a middle-aged Afro-American female celebrity
        who's visiting their rust belt town,
recently photographed
        on the arm of a young stud
at her newsworthy cultural happening, who these same women

        are certain will make an appearance:
her broad and noble brow;
        chemically relaxed and straightened hair in a plain
and severe bun because
        working is practical, when you live in a right-to-work state;

her smoldering eyes are privy
to coffee break insights
their husbands and boyfriends
wipe from their faces and crumple in kerchiefs
driving home from work.

The women have no doubt she'll say to the one most
well-endowed among them,
"It was my eyes that first attracted him."

Buttocks and All, Or The European Bodybuilder

Rocky Kitchen, a dedicated bodybuilding trainee, had plenty of time to visualize his future chest development during the three hundred mile round trip he made from Vero Beach three times a week.

Several of our staff noticed Rocky was finally getting discouraged, and had an idea. The latest European bodybuilding magazine had just arrived. Its cover showed a bodybuilder from the waist up, his hands behind his head.

"I've got an idea," said one of the staff. "We have some photos around here of a pair of heavy set female buttocks which we were planning on using in a hip-slimming article. We can cut out the chest cover and place the buttocks behind the cover, where they'll project through. Then we'll make a print of the entire picture, buttocks and all!"

The new cover was prepared. The fellows in on the joke were amazed at how real it looked. The European bodybuilder now had the thickest pectoral muscles in history.

"It makes Ross and Eifferman look like flat-chested girls," somebody said.

The big moment arrived. Rocky drove up as usual in the late afternoon. "Hey Rocky!" said one of the fellows. "We've finally got the new chest machine built and we've been secretly testing it in Europe. Take a look at one of the trainees."

"Damnation," Rocky replied as he stared at the picture. "Those are the thickest pecs I've ever seen. Book me on the next flight to Europe."

D'Accord

Black Econoline
panel van
leaves the parking lot and
slowly crawling
scales my field of vision,
a fizzing squib of sunlight fixed
to the luggage rack
the pedestrian overpass hiccups.

In a building
made to break apart in sections
in case of an earthquake
a janitor
can't pronounce the name I can't remember
for the third, no,
wait a minute, fourth time.
Our agreement
lodged where you can't find it
driving your windowless van on a stretch of unfinished
rural road: no reduced
speed ahead
highway signs
as far back as you remember.

D'accord:
not to let on in front of this
janitor,

and all the others like him.
The name he is looking right through me for
I finally realize isn't a name at all,

but rather some antlered thing
from which neither of us will ever
disentangle.
The girl who's off to the side buying some blonde fudge.
I want to know
who's to say to no one

in particular
she doesn't know my heart's desire, and who will overhear.
When she approaches.

I don't have to slow down here, do I?

The Galactic Herald of Daedalus Goes Shopping for an Engagement Ring, and Settles on the Perverse, Adolescent Genius of the Wenger Giant Pocketknife

"The smallest units of matter are not physical objects in the ordinary sense;
they are forms, ideas which can be expressed unambiguously only in
mathematical language."
—Werner Heisenberg

The silver body paint
Mother bought and applied to me
streaks and runs black.
Another needle breaks off deep
in my shoulder.
The oily suspension
requires a bigger gauge.
Anyway,
Mother's no good at injecting.
An orange smear where she swabs my arm with
a cotton ball,
the smell of rubbing alcohol
tickles my nose.
I'm unsteady on metal casters as Mother leads me
down the aisle of shadow box displays angled like a saber arch or
A-frame overhead,
where laid out on green felt Swiss army knives
have been mounted according to size, from the larger below to
the smaller above. The ones at the apex
achieve the sublime, a Platonic ideal of the multitool,
manifold function distilled to an essence,
a question of how you decide
between tweezers, a lens, and file, or scissors, hook,
and reamer, punch with sewing eye….
What algorithmic mystery of usefulness and need
the design of each knife suggests.
Totally different from
the old-school
analog synth on the counter.
Tweak a knob, and the sound from one
key depressed, making sound

at a time will change.
Could have only one yellowed plastic key,
with endless dials and buttons to marshal a galaxy of sound.
A pistol grip drill in her delicate, plump hand,
Mother gently revs the motor,
to spin the chuck.
Her other hand swabbing my temple she says,
"Now,
that one is a real gem."

Bolstering

Scooting away from us
to the far
side of the mattress
the inventor
kicks off the covers,
the bed sheets and comforter,
settling in next to the cinderblock wall.
Lindsay stuffs another pillow
behind my back and asks if 'nooners' are always like this.
Lindsay was a child star. She spent one
summer vacation from primary school on a log
raft, floating down a river, Robert Mitchum swatting her ass
for over-enunciating bad lines....
Well you know what they say about child stars.
She came to the premier as Robert's escort, candy on his arm.
So this, tonight,
for myself and the others who
have gathered here,
is good.
I mean, I'm grateful she's willing to mount and ride cowgirl.
But this isn't the Special Olympics;
not everybody wins.
I have to get better
before Lindsay's prayers
are answered.
Wondering whether she knows
that to care for a person bestows him a hostage to fate,
I remember how trying to spot constellations
at night with my father, I heard
something like cracks in the ice of a pond
frozen in winter. Then he asked me,
"Which stars will you use to distribute your weight?"

Apollonian Bag Gloom Brew

I like to walk around at night.
I like my clothes as roomy as I can get them.
Gripped in a lifestyle these preferences gather around me
what majesty
a desolate basketball court projects:
the gentle curving backboard reminds me of a headboard
of a bed I slept in
before another person's couch
and some foil and thumbtacks—to cover the only window….
The imprints little stars
in relief on the heads of the tacks
leave on the tips of my fingers: my quavery hand
shakes my arm to vibrate
in my shoulder. Axillary nodes aren't
any more painful to have taken out than other nodes,
raising your arm will just hurt worse than hell, after the biopsy.
Waking up
on sweaty, pilled acrylic foam cushions,
pinpricks of sun
spilled on wooden floorboards….
Stinging scalp,
yanked-out hairs
wound tight around fingers,
I start to wonder if there ever was a reason to
be unhappy, if you even were.

The Soul of This Poem Is My Blood Sugar, Or Eating in the Small Room

for John Cassavetes

Tippi Hedren could be more at a loss than me,
or you—
I can't remember who
is whom—but she's playing herself,
hosting *Dinner and a Movie...The Birds* on cable, see?
It's the first time she's worked in ages and
who could blame her?
A chance
like Hitchcock afforded
only comes along once, sometimes,
and who needs more than that to ruin a career?
Not established like Stewart, or typecast like Perkins or Leigh,
she can still be counted on for earnest.
But sincere is no kind of disguise—
you don't even know who's on the level
in our business.
All we do know
is everything that's in our frame isn't all we're here for.
I've got some kind of blood
disease,
has to do with sugar,
either too much or too little—
I can't remember but I've got to eat
every couple of hours:
green salads and whey protein shakes,
amino acids and tomato juice.
Eating myself, bright-eyed and fit, into the zone.

Let's say I take a risk
and fail,
who's going to be there for me?
Who will take care of little Miss Jenny Rowlands?

Sibilance

Poor enormous Lou Ferrigno
just wants to help.
Or was he practicing his lines?

More rangy than he looked in the old series, my mom looks
at him, and back to me, as the big fellow approaches
and throws down a standardized test answer book like it's some
kind of gauntlet: the cover unfolding: my name in chicken
scratches, rows of addition.

My dad is out.
If he comes from the north,
through the breezeway,
and I'm still here...

Number two
pencils
scattered around
the tips of his gleaming brogues,
what is dad
going to offer in trade for
the jocular elbowing walk past the bike rack?

III. Coils

Hyde: Get back to your piano! Go on!
Jekyll's Mother: I beg of you sir! My fingers are numb!
Hyde: All the better. Play a march!

Docteur Jekyll et Les Femmes (1981)
Dir. Walerian Borowczyk

May 1976

Father works at his lathe,
crank-handles capped with yellow plastic.
The shuttered garage door
raised up
as high as his shoulders.
Rain drizzles and beads on oily blacktop smeared with
a sheen like colored cellophane.

The dowels become
thinner. He stands them in a five-gallon bucket.
His eyes are small.

He secures each dowel in serrated jaws of an iron vise,
marking the dowels with a see-through
mechanical pencil.

He sets me down
on the stepladder, hangs the saw
from a ten-penny nail, beside the cut of plywood
shaped like a peanut shell.

Gathers pegs up off the floor.
Claps his hands,
and brushes sawdust from
dark trouser legs.

Traveler's creases like plumb lines
on the front of his pants,
Father's standing like there's a pebble in
one or both

of his wingtip brogues
and he doesn't want to move around
anymore.

The Culture of Milling

Fifty years for the bakery, the little guy's bakery in the barbecue capital of the world. Working all day on precarious legs. A comment that was routine to hear was he worked so much because at home the moat was drawn. Once I heard someone call his home a suitcase castle. Someone behind a customer who was picking up an order uttered the words "suitcase castle." An insulated mug dangling from his utility belt, the customer before me looked like a laborer on his morning break. As he removed a check folded in half from the pocket of his insulated puffer vest, I noticed the check was already filled out. When I notice the price on the check is different from the price I quoted, I wait until what must seem to him the last possible moment before mentioning the discrepancy—it's common for the wealthy to have their servants and laborers run their errands, many of them sheltered their whole lives, afraid to walk the streets with so much as a blank check. No one blames them, least of all their laborers and other people in their employ, people like this guy, his indignation at, and contempt for this clerk, and by association the wispy-legged man about whom he listened to dark gossip in line: the most righteous indignation and contempt. His employer too wary to be here and catch this spindly clerk with horn rims thumbing the scales. "Is he a miller's son?" I wondered. Millers used to be common here.

The Figurehead Has a Separate Itinerary

Carved in the sweep of a crescent facade
a statue niche
curves around and scallops overhead,
empty save for shadow no one walking past can see in

to see my white
bell-bottoms, wife beater
stained with grass, dried manure
after spending the night in the pasture
outside the city wall.

Alcoves filled with statues
reeled away,
too numerous to count
as I dashed across a deserted court
in the languid, spaghettified moment that comes with
a surge of adrenaline,
stretched to the point of translucent and arced
like a fishing line cast from a boat,
or a blemish or mote
when it nears the edge of a convex lens.

A seabreeze was blowing,
I left my coat of pilot cloth on board.

The captain at his sewing frame,
even-weave cut from bolt
embroidered with the compass and the square,
a different Sanskrit character for every member of the crew—
will he tear out the same mysterious letter
an able seaman tattooed on my back?

From other cavities pale faces gaze
not like saints
whose eyes are filled with peace and love,
nor like leaders of men,
from under strong projecting brows,
their foreheads high and broad, as resolute as ramparts,

but in horror at some distant thing
no one else can see,
that corresponds to viscera inside

stone figures that echo
dreadful secret knowledge
it's useless to deny.

Wind blusters, blows seaward.
My windbreaker flapping,
I'm colder than I think I am.

The Solution

Both Troy and I
believed
the developer's claim
that robust
asymmetric encryption
would counter my lack of decisiveness,
which had long bedeviled us.
But Troy starts
using the system to eavesdrop,
listening in
to our own conversations,
listening
by himself, later,
in private.

What Troy and I now say
to each other
with the words we carefully choose,
and the silence between our words: Troy's listening.

Maybe he's listening now.
Maybe he's listening later.

On my way to meet Troy
I wonder if I'm trying to make him believe
in the same trust we lost.
No need to prove anything, least of all to Troy,
not when it comes to selling him
the trust we lost
on the way here, to meet
for the first time.
After all, he was never there.

What's with This Anti-Touch Thing with You

Pushed away by his wife
like she's driving a stake through his heart,
a man in the corner office
of the business he built from scratch
asks her, "What's the deal with this anti-touch
thing with you?" Patting his sternum,
she gives him a look like he shouldn't have said that
and leaves.

Each appointment
shorter
than the one before, there's so little time
he thinks
as he crosses legs
and swivels his high wingback chair,

with the tip of his brogue
pushes closed a panel desk drawer,
listening
to the sound of it slide:
heavy and sluggish with folders yet
smooth,
without friction,
on ball bearing-filled rollers.

Sun through metal blinds emerging
sharp and afternoonish,
he hears

someone
say, "I guess it wasn't
me all those years ago, or yesterday, even."

He corrects invoices
long into that first night

Study for a Portrait as Polarities

Legs in white crocheted floral tights,
and bare in navy Eton shorts and knee high socks,
dangle through delicate potbelly curve
of the wrought iron rail,
to swing
back and forth,
toddlers' feet in black
patent gloss
Mary Janes, saddle shoes
trimmed with brogue, high above
blonde
parquet floor
splashed with color
from light through lead
crystal panes
set in a heavy oaken door, his children on the balcony,
left on their own in the funeral parlor,
where the corpse of their father is now on display:
small hands that clutch iron
flared like the shape of woman who's pregnant and carries
the child low on her abdomen,
late in her term,
holding the bars of the parents' mistake,
a deceased father's last thought the next thing you know.

I Believe You

Said
what you said. And beyond that,
not much.
The resulting sadness
concentrates my self-awareness,
at the same time
smashing it into abundant refractions that dazzle like afternoon sun
I enter squinty-eyed
after drinking in a darkened corner of the bar all morning,
the sequined bodice of day
gaudy and overexposed through a tangle of eyelashes.
What the taste of chocolate frosting
waxy with
too much paraffin does
to every thought you have about
cake.
Often I'm able to
reason backwards from a proposition, or at least discover
the murky origin
in a far recess of a stranger's unconscious,
but with all this talk,
what was it?
Something about bears,
hypothetically tracking them…not.
I've got to stop. I mean,
it's a clear day.
Prowling the lowlands while dressed in this highlander
camouflage,
when I look up and see not a cloud in a sky
torn to scraps and swatches beyond the leafy canopy,
it means there's little to no chance of torrential
rain and all it drenches
helping a profile that's optically fractured and broken
but only in ways wholly conspicuous
blend in. Every tree and bush and rock formation
will continue to look
real, thus
keeping me and the ones who are watching oriented

until I ease in place, slide and
come to rest
at the apex where myriad crosshairs converge.

Looking Out over Their Heads for the First Time

The whole gymnasium notes the trophy
unsteady on casters.
Metal bleachers wheeze as people crane and lean.
The dowager prods her husband to talk
about "that thing"
that always intrigued him.
Sitting next to you their daughter contracts.

Breccia Lens, Or Moonlight Feathers the Nest of a Woman with Her Throat Cut

Broken off
above the blackened rim,
my ribs
white as teeth.
Arranged in a halo
about my head
men stood,
and with hands and arms
gestured in different directions.
It's so
polished and smooth
I thought
beholding my cauterized, scraped-out chest
cavity,
stars shining down
from beyond the colonial house frame.

Relationship to the Mysterious Object of Desire Expressed as a Configuration of Triangles

So I either like all women the same, I mean a lot,
or I hate cute, defenseless animals,
like the baby harp seal in an animal-rights campaign,
flat charcoal eyes and nose stuck on the pinched-off end of curving
white loaf like a soft serve turd. The latter inference
helpful in quiet
subject to
transformation,
like carpet whorls
making the shape of a Midwestern state.
Always the same state—
no matter where I go, I can't escape
This state
that produces wheat and pumpjacks.
Wheat grew your buttocks full and round and clad in blue denim,
until you pushed the denim down
over your hips, your thighs, around your ankles, stepping out of it.
We call that exporting.
You export denim and dreams, dreams
I dream of spanking you
with a clear Lexan paddle drilled with ten bevel-edged holes
equidistant,
arranged in a triangle,
dreams of spanking you I import.
The denim made me keep importing dreams,
more and more dreams, even after the market was glutted.
Now in repose on wooden slats
that straighten around an axis of spring eleven times a day
like the hands on an analog clock,
winding me tighter and tighter until you are
all that remains where the luxury cruise liner deckchair
you reclined on,
at your leisure, for my pleasure,
used to be: your pale
skin yet emblazoned with lines
from the bars of the cage my desire makes.

Three Tits Calligraphy

Fewer nerve endings per square inch on your back
than…elsewhere, let's say,
so the character the tiny metal sphere of a ballpoint pen,
rolling, scraping dryly in its socket,
carves in skin there on your back lays down a
flagstone of sensation
to become a winding garden path of
goose flesh
that tingles like a lit black powder fuse,
or a slinking feathered boa, seeping up your nape and over
the base of your skull as viscous ink
conveyed by capillary action
streaks and staggers in the waxy sebum,
your broad, turtle-shell back
aroused, on life turned,
hunched over round shoulders:
every line, every stroke
hopelessly, and completely disperses.

Course of Desire

In the silent worship of another's body
that follows an encounter
best described as
by proxy,
the bouncers' lonely calls
drift up like smoke through the floorboards.
Walking up the stairs outside the bar,
in the dark between
open-riser plywood steps
I made out eyes reflecting light.
When she opens her mouth as if to speak
dread rips through me
like lightning through a thunderhead;
at the end of her pale, willowy leg a gold and silver
embroidered house slipper gleams.

Untitled

Sweat on the side of our double old-fashioned rocks glasses
attracting a hornet as big as my thumb,
Marie grabs her cold drink, a white napkin dark grey with damp,
stuck to the beveled octagonal side.

A trapezoid-shaped flower bed
filled with river-culled orange rock and edged
with monkey grass,
a burned-up match on the concrete,
next to Marie's bare foot.

Phone receiver squashing my ear, index
finger-twined springy cord
cutting off circulation, on the other end
someone has put the handset
down with a muted, percussive thud,
like the sound it would make
set on a note pad, or desk calendar.
Behind the brown refrigerator
door ice
slips in the ice-maker.
Marie looks up and exhales smoke
and resumes waving away flies
trying to get at the steaks she has covered with cling wrap.

"What an asshole," she says, and then bridles,
her blonde hair
tangled and caught in the spines of the holly behind her.

The Rhythm of Things

The cactus gestures with a slender, spiny branch
from its red pot.
"This is for flowers," it hisses,
taunting purple bean pods.
The purple bean pods have nothing to say.
Twisted, curled, withered, dry,
they have nothing to say. Scattered
on the white bookcase,
stems like burnt matchsticks.
The cactus keeps at it: poking the hulls
and making threats.
I can't tell if they're used to this treatment or not.
The bean pods are models.
Lindsay gathers them behind the grocery store,
on the dirt path
that leads to railroad tracks.
In her paintings
they're two or three feet long and yellow, brown, or blue.

What does the cactus want?
Why don't the pods resist?
The cactus rears back and winds up
as if to strike
with a branch I take hold of to break off a spine.
On the tip of my thumb
a drop of blood
expands, and heavy, runs.

Standing in the doorway
Lindsay twists a fork in a plate of spaghetti,

noodles stained
bright tomato-paste red,
metal tines
scraping the glaze.

Elephant Fords River

The living room
empty except for packing boxes
with canted open flaps,
wads of newsprint shaped like visceral fat,
Zoe picks at pale green carpet,
square and matted
darkly shaded where the coffee table leg dug in,
and sprawls, raising up a knee
under the stretched-out, gaping hem
of her black evening gown
that leers,
a manic grin I crawl inside,
lurching forward awkward and ungainly,
invertebrate
as a concertina bellows
to rut between
Zoe's splayed open thighs,
both my eyes
shut in the dark underneath a photographer's hood
where the aperture of my memory
to a pinpoint constricts,
casting our rapidly vanishing present
as it becomes
past
in the sharpest of focus.

How I Imagine You Now

The pause mechanism
having run out of time allotted to
view any single frame
before the video player enters sleep mode,
and the tv,
lacking signal or source,
leaves me
with a vivid blue screen,
that's not unlike the chroma key green,
the unique and distinct and as far from the natural
skin tone
of humans as possible
green hue
the punk rocker-turned-actor
spoke lines and
gestured in front of as guest
on a lesbian's daytime variety talk show,
a green set that
later became animated
interior barn,
as the audience watched
the ex-rocker
perform, perfectly
execute
deep knee bends,
back straight and head held up,
muscular thighs parallel
to the floor
sprinkled with hay,
with his ass jutting out to catch
the loosened snow that falls from a rafter,
before he shakes it off and looks
over his shoulder,
annoyed as a duck in cartoons,
looking at something or someone not me,
who was
then yanking
stained mattress

ticking
from beneath my latest conquest,
a woman I'd just realized I didn't desire, and in fact
probably wouldn't, the mere possibility
of some later remorse only a vulgar absurdity, present tinnitus
excepted, of course…
I recall the idea that presented itself
while I watched you unwrap
in the sun and then bite at the marketing ploy
known as half-a-footlong
and set it down on the concrete.

Leg

Panel the color of raw
steak discoloring
once it's exposed to the air
slides on its runner, crosscutting fibres
bunched into fascicles sheathed with elastin
that shift like amoebas, contract, clinch,
then dilate again.
Panel
after panel,
runners underfoot and
thickness of panels decreasing.
A click,
something catches.
Or caught,
something releases
and scrapes to the opposite wall.
This fleshly corridor
can't go on much longer:
the panels can get no thinner.
The thought of hiding
once I'm out,
the reason not to hide.
Never did I present agoraphobia,
or tendencies…say,
vampiric.
No symptoms of anemia.
Never was a bleeder,
in any sense.
I have to keep my nerve.
It's all that separates me from
my surroundings.
My leg
feels…feels like.

Acknowledgments

Indiana Review ("Your Face Burns My Hands")
Curbside Splendor ("The Tang")
Heavy Feather Review ("Tuning")
MAYDAY ("The Galactic Herald Of Daedalus Goes Shopping For An Engagement Ring")
CrossConnect ("Still Life With Human Beings," "How I Imagine You Now")
Poetry Quarterly ("Looking Out Over Their Heads For The First Time")
REAL: Regarding Arts and Letters ("The Story Of The Matte Kind, Or Road," "The Renowned Cinematographer Shows Off On His Honeymoon," "Bolstering," "May, 1976," "Breccia Lens, Or Moonlight Feathers The Nest Of A Woman With Her Throat Cut")
Sierra Nevada Review ("Dismember, Or The Swimmer At Land")
Blastfurnace ("Travelers Dream About The Peasants")
Dr. T. J. Eckleburg Review ("Mary And Barb")
Literary Juice ("First Course In Etiquette")
Line Zero ("Course of Desire")
Black Heart Magazine ("Sibilance")
Sugar Mule ("Blue Cannibals," "Untitled [Reflected]" "Poached," "Apollonian," "Three Tits Calligraphy")
Former People: A Journal of Bangs and Whimpers ("The Figurehead Has A Separate Itinerary," "Caravan")
Contraposition ("Elephant Fords River")
Forge ("What's With This Anti-Touch Thing With You")
Riverrun ("The Rhythm Of Things")
Tule Review ("Untitled")
pifmagazine ("Portrait As A Study For Polarities") *Rockhurst Review* ("Portrait As A Study For Polarities")
The Antigonish Review ("Arboreal Is As Close As I Can Get To Her")
Bangalore Review ("The Soul Of This Poem Is My Blood Sugar, Or Eating In The Small Room")

Poesis ("Voix Acousmatique Overheard By A Pilgrim With Skin In The Game," "The Mysterious Object Of Desire Expressed As A Configuration Of Triangles," "Course Of Desire")
The Floor Plan ("Security," "Buttocks And All, Or The European Bodybuilder," "The Solution," "I Believe You") *Piker Press* ("Broadside")